GREAT CENTRAL RAILWAY

DECLINE AND FALL

John Evans

AMBERLEY

First published 2020

Amberley Publishing
The Hill, Stroud
Gloucestershire, GL5 4EP

www.amberley-books.com

Copyright © John Evans, 2020

The right of John Evans to be identified as the
Author of this work has been asserted in accordance
with the Copyrights, Designs and Patents Act 1988.

ISBN 978 1 4456 9557 0 (print)
ISBN 978 1 4456 9558 7 (ebook)

British Library Cataloguing in Publication Data.
A catalogue record for this book is available from
the British Library.

Typeset in 9.5pt on 12.2pt Celeste.
Origination by Amberley Publishing.
Printed in the UK.

Introduction

The Great Central Railway touches the emotions like few other lines. As a complete entity it existed for only sixty-seven years, but it had a unique character and engendered huge pride among those employed on it. I was lucky enough to know it at the end of its more prosperous days and then through the increasingly sad sixties, when the London Midland Region sucked the heart out of it like a corporate vampire. Had it survived a few more years, it might have become a key part of the nation's transport infrastructure, the role that its promoter Sir Edward Watkin envisaged for it.

That was not to be. Now it exists as a grim scar across the countryside and in odd remains of structures in towns and cities through which it passed. It is quite salutary to think that the vast viaducts that swept over Leicester and Nottingham have been largely removed. Imagine the effort it took to create them. In true modern corporate strategic planning fashion, of course, the bridge over Nottingham Midland station was removed, then one was required after all, so a replacement has been installed.

This book takes as its subject the ten years from 1963, when the line was still in fine form and busy with freight and passenger traffic (especially with excursion trains on summer weekends). For some unplanned reason Woodford Halse is a recurring theme. It concludes in 1973. Why 1973? Well, it was a year of endings and beginnings. The demolition men had already inflicted a vast amount of damage and yet the new Great Central Railway heritage line took its first tentative steps towards creating the fine reminder of erstwhile glory that it is today.

I could not have created this tribute without the help of the photographers who have given me such free access to their precious collections. Thanks also to Bryan Jeyes, who witnessed closely the physical destruction of Nottingham Victoria – one of the finest stations outside London – and then walked all the way from there to Rugby Central. He also kindly read the text. Thanks to Graham Onley for putting the railway in context; to Rob Govier who takes us back to the current railway's frail beginnings; and to all others who offered advice and guidance. I am also grateful to the *Northampton Chronicle and Echo* for permission to reprint two articles about the Great Central which, written so many years ago, give an emotional and social dimension to this depressing story. The text of this book was written by me, except where credited.

The modernist writer Ford Madox Ford opens his novel *The Good Soldier* with the words: 'This is the saddest story I have ever heard.' He might have been writing about the latter days of the Great Central.

John Evans
Luddenden,
2020

Great Central – Decline and Fall

It is a freezing Sunday afternoon in January 1967. We are travelling west over snowy country lanes from our home in Northampton to pay our last respects to an old friend – the Great Central Railway. The word is out that the demolition men are approaching, and this could be our final chance to see one of its key stations intact. The light is already starting to fade as we pull up outside the deserted station entrance, a modest door in a wall. Happily, that door is open. No trains will come, and nobody cares any more.

We climb the stairs up to the impressive island platform and head to the south end of the station. Ahead of us, the two main lines sweep into the distance underneath an elegant arched bridge, shrouded by a shallow cutting typical of those on the southern section of the old Great Central. Everything is covered in a blanket of white. A large bracket signal has lost its arms; a water crane has filled its last tender. There are indentations in the snow where sidings have been removed. The signal box is silent. In fact, that is the eeriest thing – the absolute silence as the snow muffles any distant sounds. Off to the right, a spur provides a link to the one-time Stratford-upon-Avon & Midland Junction Railway. Who would have thought that ramshackle enterprise would last as long as the Great Central that was so important in feeding it? Now both are doomed. The strange wooden platform that once served local trains to Stratford and the footbridge that links it to the rest of the station have not been used for some time – the snow is deep and unmarked. We climb the footbridge steps for a view north, where there is still a labyrinth of lines, but nothing resembling the huge marshalling yards that only a few years earlier were busy day and night. We are not the only ones to have visited the north end, as the platforms have a trail of footprints in the snow. After a short while and with darkness approaching, we pack away our cameras. Soon, everything we see, built to last generations, will be rubble. We spot a flash of red in the undergrowth, a redundant signal arm. We pick it up and take it home. That, our photographs and our memories are our only reminders today of Woodford Halse.

No trains today. A freezing day at Woodford Halse in January 1967, four months after closure.
(John Evans)

On the Right Lines

Enthusiasts living in Northamptonshire in the 1960s enjoyed the benefit of five main lines passing northwards through their county. From the East Coast Main Line, at Peterborough, to the Great Western route from Oxford to Birmingham, at King's Sutton, there was a unique choice of locations for those wishing to spend summer Saturdays watching trains in the sunshine. For many of us living in the county town, a quick push-pull ride to Blisworth or Bedford was enough. But Northampton also had regular services to Rugby, and that meant access to the most mysterious and furtive of those five main lines – the Great Central.

Because it passed through just the small market town of Brackley and a host of villages, the Great Central seldom appeared on our radar, although we had an idea that there was a freight shed of some importance at Woodford Halse. Without car transport, reaching Woodford from Northampton was a challenge of multiple bus routes not worth contemplating. But Rugby – well, that sounded a much better bet. So one morning in 1959, instead of the usual 5-mile trip to Blisworth on the West Coast Main Line, we bought half returns to Rugby Midland. On arrival at its cavernous island platform, we found some fellow spotters, who advised us to head for a field just south of the famous girder bridge that swept the Great Central across the town, a site which also gave a view of all other train movements.

The first Great Central working we saw was a northbound freight headed by a B16 4-6-0. Shortly afterwards came an L1 tank on a local, and then the first of many 9F-hauled freights. By the end of the day we had witnessed a whole host of previously unseen engines, from K3s and V2s to more familiar types, but with unfamiliar numbers. We even saw a couple of Great Western locomotives. The sheer variety of motive power was overwhelming, especially when coupled to the intense summer Saturday activity on the West Coast Main Line. It was too good to last.

By 1966, when the Great Central was closed south of Rugby and its status as a main line destroyed, I had managed to travel over all of it, from Marylebone to Manchester, although in three chunks rather than one continuous run on a through express. On the final day of operations, 3 September 1966, I went to Brackley to see a last day special. After it raced south over one of the wonderful viaducts that helped to give the line its sweeping alignment, there was little to do but go home and contemplate the intricacies of railway politics that led to the best-engineered main line in Britain falling to the demolition man's axe.

In the early 1970s I moved to live within a couple of miles of the old GC's trackbed, by then fighting a desperate battle against nature and developers. Cities like Leicester and Nottingham were changed in their very nature as the vast bridges and viaducts of the Great Central were removed. The gently sloping cuttings were filled with undergrowth or worse, stations were demolished and even Nottingham Victoria, surely the finest station in the Midlands, was unceremoniously battered by ball and chain until just the clock tower remained, isolated like a gaunt and sad reminder of something once great. Now it is surrounded by modern buildings in a setting that could hardly be less cohesive.

The decline and fall of the Great Central happened quickly and irreverently. In 1959 you could catch some of the finest, fleetest trains in the country. It was also a shining example of how to move freight. Ten years later the section between Nottingham and Aylesbury was gone and a mammoth scar across the countryside was the only reminder of Sir Edward Watkin's great vision of a high-speed railway line that would eventually connect with the Channel Tunnel.

The revival of a section between north Leicester and south Nottingham is one of the triumphs of railway preservation. But this book is not really about preservation; it tells the story in essays and pictures of the last years of the Great Central – mainly the closed section between Nottingham and Aylesbury – and the sad obliteration of some of its principal features.

Its proud and positive motto was 'Forward'. What a shame that the London Midland Region of British Railways, which was responsible for closing it, did not have the same progressive approach.

A Black 5 waits to move stock out of Rugby Central in 1965. Two years later there would be buffer stops in the distance after the tracks south were hastily removed. (John Evans)

The London Extension – A Journey in Words

The Great Central neatly divided itself into five parts, each with a rather different character. Starting from Marylebone, there was the first 38-mile stretch to Aylesbury. Then came the very rural section to Rugby. After that, trains headed through busier territory to Nottingham Victoria, before travelling to Sheffield over lines hemmed in by collieries and busy towns. From Sheffield Victoria, the final section pointed westwards across the Pennines on electrified lines to Manchester. We are going to take a ride on the section north to Nottingham, just as it was in the early 1960s.

The so-called London Extension had a fairly complicated history and with Metropolitan line trains running alongside the Great Central rails, initially it was very much a London suburban route. Aylesbury itself, where you often found a local to Princes Risborough waiting in the station, boasted three platforms and a bell tower on the roof. You can still inspect the LNER-built station at Aylesbury (or Aylesbury Town as it used to be known), but not the small engine shed that was closed in 1962. Once north of Aylesbury, the nature of the line to Rugby started to change. The stations were shared with the Metropolitan Railway as far as Quainton Road, where there was a very attractive rustic branch line to Brill. The landscape was leafy and gently undulating, but at the remote hamlet of Calvert there was a brickworks. Calvert station was the first station heading north that followed the very characteristic format of an island platform with buildings nestling against an overbridge.

This layout was economical to build and allowed for fast running. Usually there was a siding or two, perhaps loops or a modest goods yard. Access for passengers was through a small entrance hall, with steps descending (or in one or two cases, ascending) to the platform. Here you found a compact booking office. Each station was slightly different but was unmistakably a Great Central London Extension building. The Great Central was also economical with its provision of covered awnings; if you wanted access to the waiting room, a separate building, and it was raining, you'd get wet. Once into Buckinghamshire, and especially in Northamptonshire, the wide cuttings, extensive viaducts and country stations serving small populations proved a very attractive alternative for photographers used to the West Coast and Great Western main lines, neither of which was very far away.

Continuing north, after important links to Verney Junction and Ashendon Junction, we arrive at Finmere. This station had had its busy times, but by the 1960s those days were over – save for term-related traffic from nearby Stowe School. It closed in 1963 during the London Midland Region's pre-Beeching cull of Great Central local stations. Next came

Brackley Central, a fairly impressive station, but still conforming to the island platform concept, with steps leading down from a well-designed booking hall, which still exists.

Helmdon, even today, has fewer than a thousand residents. Helmdon for Sulgrave station (the suffix being an attempt to attract visitors to George Washington's ancestral home a couple of miles from the station) closed in 1963.

Culworth served where? Well, perhaps the village of Moreton Pinkney. It was on a very spacious site with bridges at either end. This station was closed in 1958, only surviving the nearby Towcester to Stratford-upon-Avon line's other Moreton Pinkney station by seven years. Both stations were actually well situated to serve the village; a pity that the village was always tiny, with limited revenue potential – even today it only has 400 residents. The railway then arrived at Woodford Halse, which is the subject of discussion elsewhere in this narrative.

Charwelton offered the chance to see traffic being marshalled to and from the local ironstone quarry. There was then a lengthy rural stretch along the Northamptonshire/Warwickshire border through the 3,000-yard Catesby Tunnel until the tall masts of Rugby wireless transmitting station came into distant view and trains arrived at Braunston and Willoughby. Like Culworth, three stations on this section were at locations already served by rail – Helmdon, on the sleepy Towcester to Banbury route; Brackley, on the somewhat busier and more important line from Bletchley to Banbury; and Braunston and Willoughby, which was already served by a station on the fascinating and often ignored Weedon to Leamington route. Braunston and Willoughby (the station was nearer Willoughby) was also shut before the closure of most Great Central local stations in 1963: in fact, the village lost both its stations in a sixteen-month period between 1957 and 1958. At most of these Northamptonshire locations, the Great Central competed for what we might call modest traffic potential.

Those people living in the first half of the twentieth century at the small villages of Moreton Pinkney, Helmdon and Willoughby may consider themselves very fortunate to have lived for so long with two stations each to serve them, with a rich variety of destinations. For the Great Central it was less beneficial: did they ever make a profit from them? Yet what could be nicer than setting off north along this line with an L1 2-6-4 tank and a few coaches, savouring the English countryside uninterrupted by the pressures of having to share your compartment with another passenger? On some trains you could have a whole coach to yourself.

And so we move to the section from Rugby to Nottingham, a much more remunerative area for the GC line and, indeed, the only section to survive the London Extension closure programme in 1966. As you approached Rugby you could see huge mounds of earth grassed over; this was the spoil removed when the cuttings through Rugby were excavated.

Rugby Central was hardly a glamorous station. The booking hall with its three gables was mounted on an angled bridge over the railway and you descended through a rather tatty covered stairway to reach the platforms. The buildings were similar to most other island platform stations on the GC. The sidings were in use right to the end, as a morning local from Leicester had to be shunted across to the Down side to allow the semi-fast from Nottingham to use the Up platform. After setting off north through a cutting, the railway passed over the West Coast Main Line on a lengthy girder bridge, which also passed the locomotive testing station created jointly by the LNER and LMS and was destined for a fairly short life. Frustratingly, there was no connection between the Great Central and West Coast main lines. The LNWR would argue it did not need one. It already had a direct Midland Railway route from Rugby to Leicester (and a rather more tortuous way of reaching Brackley and Aylesbury). The GC then ran on an embankment north-eastward and it was quite surprising to see the speed of passenger trains on this section, especially those that were about to call, or had just called, at Rugby Central.

The first station after Rugby was Lutterworth, which was reached by stairs from the street below. Lutterworth was a small Leicestershire town – not much more than a village – when served by the Great Central. Today its population is heading towards 10,000 and would well justify a station. We are now on the part that survived the initial closure of the London Extension, but in its last three years, travelling on a diesel multiple unit between Rugby and Nottingham was a depressing experience. North of Lutterworth, the GC's proximity was invaded by a new intruder – the M1 motorway. I can clearly recall watching the building work advance as we travelled in the mid-1960s. The line ran through cuttings and then a short tunnel before reaching Ashby Magna, a tiny village of a couple of hundred people.

This was a delightful part of south Leicestershire. Ashby Magna station had a tall signal at its south end but was otherwise standard Great Central. We once got off here and grabbed a photograph of the engine, just to say we had been there. Then we hopped back on the same train as the guard stood impatiently waiting (we had left the door open to make sure he didn't go without us). Nobody else joined or alighted, yet it survived the 1963 cull of stations on this section.

Drive up the M1 today and you will pass beneath a sturdy steel bridge as you approach Leicester. This carried the GC over the M1 where it swung right and headed towards the next station, Whetstone. You were now on the outskirts of Leicester in a village, and although its population was small, the district around it today has a population of 120,000. It was also served by the Birmingham to Leicester line, which is still open. Whetstone was a standard GC station with access from below, but it was another casualty of early closures, shutting its doors in March 1963. I seem to recall this station still being intact for many years after closure, although it was one we never visited. After passing above the lines from Leicester to Rugby and Birmingham, the GC crossed the River Soar on a splendid viaduct and ran through the outskirts of the city alongside the busy goods yard at Leicester South Goods. On the Up side was Leicester locomotive shed, which, despite its impecunious appearance, had housed A3 Pacifics in the 1950s, and then V2s. The Leicester London Road to Burton line crossed the GC just south of the shed. Leicester North Goods yard was passed shortly before trains ran across a splendid bow string viaduct and entered Leicester Central.

This was a huge island platform, true to GC philosophy. It had bays at both ends and on summer Saturdays the procession of through trains requiring an engine change made it a spotter's paradise. It was handsome from the exterior, too, with a modest clock tower and elegant Dutch-style architecture, much of which survives to this day. There was a servicing area with a turntable – it was not unusual for trains arriving from the south, hauled by Western Region engines, to turn and quickly be sent home either light engine, or hauling a local. This station gradually faded away, ending up as a vast unstaffed halt with much of it shut off to passengers. We were regulars at Leicester City football matches in the old days, and over the years gradually watched the GC disintegrate from being a landmark that cut through the city to virtually invisible, unless you were in the know. Trains headed away across further viaducts and bridges with more yards until passing Belgrave Cemetery and reaching Belgrave and Birstall. This was an attractive station in a cutting, to usual GC standards; it was also a casualty of the 1963 closure programme. The new Great Central Railway chose to build a new station (Leicester North) here as the southern point of their operations from Loughborough. The old entrance to Belgrave and Birstall can be seen a short distance north of the new station. The attractive scenery in this area tempted the preservationists to select the route to Loughborough for their new project. There were also two big cities to offer potential customers and is now, of course, a major regional tourist attraction.

The first station after Belgrave and Birstall is Rothley. Of a standard GC design, it was also closed in 1963, but its wonderful restoration would defy the impression that it had ever been derelict. In fact, it was shut for twelve years. North of Rothley was a branch to Mountsorrel quarry, before the line passes over Swithland Reservoir, today the scenic high point on the revived Great Central line's journey. The next station is Quorn and Woodhouse, another amazing restoration. I took a party of people for dinner on the line for my fiftieth birthday and we were invited to leave the train at Quorn and to sample the atmosphere on a misty late November night. Strolling around under gas lamps sipping a glass or two was something very special, so Quorn holds a unique place in my heart. I also managed to scrounge a cab ride back to Loughborough on B1 No. 1264! Not a bad evening at a station that left the national network in 1963, but whose afterlife has proved much more impressive.

One of the great stations of the heritage railway world is Loughborough Central. It is also another one where we leapt off, took photos and then clambered back on board (the guard was getting used to us by now). From the exterior it is not too impressive but walk down to the platforms and you find a station that is a cut above most other GC islands, with long platforms and a busy yard. In the old days the station name boards announced you should alight for 'Loughborough College'. We live in an age where every station sign seems to be sponsored by a local university, so this was a bit of forward thinking by the town's educationalists.

Today much of the site has disappeared, including the goods yard and some sidings, but somehow the station retains the feel of its halcyon days. An interesting future awaits when instead of being the main starting point on the line, it becomes a midpoint on the journey to Ruddington.

The route now passes over the Midland main line and we would always glance to the left to see the Brush works, where the *Falcon* diesel was stored alongside the GC line in the mid-1960s. The Great Central crosses the River Soar before burrowing into the short Barnstone Tunnel and arriving at East Leake (another 'off and on' during that photographic train journey; the guard had his hands wearily on his hips as we went to work). The scenery here was always very rural and East Leake was a large village – it still is, but its population is now about 7,000 and would provide useful business if the GC had survived. It was quite busy even in the 1960s. The station had one unusual feature – a glazed and none-too-pretty covered building to protect passengers using the steps up to the platforms. East Leake survived the 1963 closures. I went back to this station in the early 1970s, but there was nothing left except a dismal platform and iron fencing around the old stairwell.

I have to confess to a complete lack of knowledge of the next station, Rushcliffe Halt, in its BR days, but I do know that unusually it had two platforms rather than the usual island style, which survive today despite its 1963 closure. The preservationists are doing all sorts of exciting things here, but our journey continues towards Nottingham past the Gotham branch to a gypsum plant and into Ruddington, another classic GC island station. A 1963 casualty, meaning our little tribe never visited it, here was a branch to a Royal Ordnance Factory. The last BR train I photographed between Aylesbury and Nottingham on the GC was a diesel heading to this factory. By this time the main line was single-track and the whole area in the kind of condition that preservation (and BR in the old days) would never have tolerated.

There was a connection to a brickworks after this, but with only a couple of chimneys it was nothing compared to Stewartby on the Bedford–Bletchley line, near where we lived. Access to Nottingham was

Bob Mullins holds the door open as I jump off our train at East Leake on a day when the guard stoically put up with our attempts to photograph several stations in one trip. (John Evans)

on four tracks crossing the River Trent on two splendid girder bridges and then passing an engine shed near Arkwright Street. Until I researched this book, I had not heard of such a building, but then I realised why; it closed in 1907. Even I am not that old, but photographs show the building was still there in the 1950s. Here also was a colliery branch and a mass of sidings forming Queen's Walk yard. Trains then entered the gloomy Nottingham Arwright Street, a High Level station that had closed in 1963 and was reopened in 1967 as the destination for diesel multiple units from Rugby. Less than two years later the London Midland Region pulled the plug, and the Great Central as a going concern was history. At least I was spared the ignominy of having seen Victoria as an unstaffed halt. It is just amazing how much of the vast array of bridges that formed the railway infrastructure in south Nottingham has disappeared. Absurdly, some of it has had to be been put back for the new tramway, Regulars on the GC in the old days will recall the excitement as you passed Weekday Cross Junction with its precarious signal box, before you plunged into the tunnel leading up to Victoria. And that was that. Your trains came out of the smokey gloom and entered a cathedral. Well, not quite, but as you will read further in this book, it was certainly something every bit as grand, if not as resolute, as the buildings the average Dean has to preside over.

From Nottingham the Great Central weaved its way north to Sheffield, competing for space with the Midland and Great Northern railways, its route originally being part of the Manchester, Sheffield & Lincolnshire Railway. The intense network of lines in north Derbyshire and Nottinghamshire served collieries and smaller towns, but while the Great Northern petered out at Langwith Junction, the Midland and GC competed for business at many towns and cities, including Chesterfield and Sheffield. Subsidence was a persistent threat, but that won't bother travellers today – they will probably be on footpaths or the 5-mile Five Pits rail trail.

The mighty Great Central bridge over Nottingham Midland station. (John Evans)

A Spotter's Delight

Nothing quite prepared the newcomer to the Great Central for the immense variety of locomotives that worked the line in its later years. Stand at Leicester Central, a major engine change point, and you could witness Great Western, BR Standard, LNER and LMS types working in harmony. A picture exists of Leicester in the late 1950s with a Cardiff Canton-based 9F on a passenger train and a gleaming 'Hall' class in the background and regulars would probably say this was nothing remarkable. In 1964, during two visits in one day to the same station, I saw all three types of London Midland Class 7P 4-6-0 - a 'Royal Scot', a 'Patriot' and a rebuilt 'Jubilee'.

In the 1950s it was very much an LNER line, with old Great Central types much in evidence, such as the A8 4-6-2 tanks, Pom Pom 0-6-0s, Robinson 2-8-0s (rebuilt and original) and even the odd 'Director' on local trains. There was also a fleet of A3 Pacifics to handle the fastest trains, but these gradually gave way to V2s, which crews reportedly preferred because their smaller driving wheels allowed better acceleration. This was the time I first remember the line, when you could see K2 and K3 2-6-0s interspersed with Standard Class 5s, B1s and V2s on expresses. But there was always the odd London Midland intruder, often Blacks 5s and 'Jubilees'. The Great Western supplied mainly Banbury-based 'Halls' on inter-regional workings, usually as far as Leicester Central, where another engine change would be made. In the last couple of years, after Leicester Central shed closed in mid-1964, the Great Western types would work through to Nottingham Victoria. The robust and effective 'Halls' never had complete dominance – you might get a 'Grange' or even a 'County' now and then.

The London Midland Region takeover eventually saw the decline of LNER types, much to the chagrin of Great Central engine men. From what I have heard about Great Central drivers (and I once spent some time with a group of retired drivers shortly after the line closed), the pecking order was clear: Eastern types were preferred; BR Standards were respected (especially the 9F); London Midland and Western types – no thank you.

Nottingham Victoria

By Bryan Jeyes

Nottingham Victoria: those two words conjure up images to so many people for a variety of reasons. Railway enthusiasts may recall magnificent locomotives in charge of trains to far flung destinations. Architectural historians will recall and bemoan the loss of yet another fine building to the concrete anonymity of twentieth-century retail development; and to some of us, in the 1960s, it was somewhere we had to visit and do our best to record while so much around us was disappearing so quickly.

I really had no idea of the depth of interest in the station and its demise until I published some of my photographs on a photo sharing site and my phone started pinging almost immediately as people – many too young to have seen the station – viewed and downloaded the images.

When preparing to compile this book, John Evans – the author – asked me to write a piece about Victoria covering its 'heady days', its last days and its demolition. The last two, melancholy though they undoubtedly are, were no problem. In the company of friend and fellow student Adam Jones – some of whose photographs appear in this book – we spent far more time there than hardworking students should have. But the heady days? I have read the books giving lists of destinations stretching from the north of the country to the South Coast, I know of the bustling local services, the summer excursions, the rail tours and, of course, the freight traffic that, amazingly, managed to negotiate the site through the station's demolition. But it's certainly not intimate knowledge.

I did visit Victoria once while through services were still running. It was in August 1965 when John and I had a 'runabout' ticket for a few days and, on this occasion, it took us from Rugby Central to Nottingham. John had visited the station before and advised me, 'You'll like Nottingham Victoria'. I was not to be disappointed. The station's lofty structure set deep in its cutting was pure drama for an unsuspecting passenger emerging from the gloom of the south tunnel. I hated the demise of steam as much as anyone, but the view from a DMU over the driver's shoulder could not be beaten. Were we arriving at one of the great London termini or a mighty religious edifice?

Roll forward just over a year and how things changed! Through services from Victoria and on the Great Central London Extension had ceased on 3 September 1966, leaving just two bay platforms in use at the station for the diesel multiple unit services to Grantham and Rugby Central. The Grantham trains were re-routed into Nottingham Midland in July 1967, leaving the cavernous Victoria effectively a large unstaffed halt for the Rugby service only.

I visited it in October of 1966. There was still some freight activity using both steam and diesel motive power, but there was hardly anybody about and the way to all parts, save the two bays, was barred by the use of the old platform benches. I remember especially two occasions from that final year. The first was a cold, dark evening in December. The huge and gloomy train shed was bathed in a gentle glow from a few platform lights. The lights of the platform 4 waiting room beckoned, and we found a small fire burning in the grate, so there must have been somebody around.

Then, in the spring of 1967, it was clear that closure could not be far off. Adam and I had a desire to record what we could of the station for the future. This was a period when Victorian buildings were not faring at all well. It was a 'bright new world' as a soap powder advert of the time said. Railway lines were closing all over the country, town centres were being ripped apart and even the magnificent St Pancras station hotel in London was surveyed ready for demolition before John Betjeman intervened just in time. We decided to take photographs, though at that time we had no idea who would see them. No internet then!

I wrote to British Railways asking for a tour of the station. I had hopes of exploring all the mysterious platform buildings but, of course, that was never going to happen. They did make someone available, however, and one afternoon in June we enjoyed a tour of all the platforms and took several colour slide photographs. The highlight was a trip up to the balcony surrounding the booking hall in the hand-powered lift. The rooms leading off the balcony were still being used by the British Transport Police at this time. What a pity we weren't taken down to the tiled subway that ran beneath the platforms.

On 4 September 1967 Nottingham Arkwright Street station – which had been closed since 1963 – was reopened as a terminus for the Rugby trains and Victoria station was closed. We weren't around at the time, as it was college vacation. We visited just ten days later, on 14 September, and couldn't believe what we saw. They had wasted no time at all; destruction was well under way. Timbers were burning alongside the platforms and the huge glass canopy adjoining the station frontage was being attacked mercilessly. Presumably it was in the way.

We visited almost every week. The photographs I took on 20 September show the front canopy gone, the main station building roof going and men tearing the train shed roof apart. This was only two weeks from closure.

There was no problem taking photos of the process: there were unobstructed views to be had of the southern platform areas from the horse dock off Glasshouse Street and the main building fronting Mansfield Road was demolished quickly, eventually giving an almost clear view of the platform buildings. When the New Theatre in Northampton was demolished, the publication *The World's Fair* said 'most theatres doomed to destruction are allowed to die decently, that is to say behind hoardings. Not so the New at Northampton.' The same could be said of Nottingham Victoria. No attempt at all was made to hide the desecration and allow the place to die quietly and with dignity out of the public gaze. Some of my photos even show someone wheeling a pram around where the tracks once were, presumably gathering something of use to them. Health and Safety considerations on demolition sites have certainly evolved since then!

Throughout the autumn of 1967 the destruction continued apace. By the end of October, barely two months after closure, most of the frontage was gone, leaving only the clock tower. Quite incredibly, my photos record that the clock was running throughout the whole of this period! Six weeks later only the central portion of the train shed, and the two main platform buildings, were left.

I took my last photograph of the demolition on 3 February 1968 because college commitments in Leicester meant I had little spare time for trips to Nottingham. By this time there wasn't a lot left, though some vestiges of the platform buildings remained holding up the Mansfield Road to Glasshouse Street footbridge.

Amazingly, limited railway operations continued through the site while the station was demolished around them. My photo of 27 September shows track lifting in progress on the east side against the Glasshouse Street wall; on 25 October we see the tracks gone and the east bay of the train shed going; then the 3 February 1968 photograph pictures the train shed gone, but newly laid tracks through the east side of the site. Many now say that failure to maintain that rail route through the new development is an opportunity missed.

I have rarely visited the Victoria Centre in recent years but on 4 September 2017 I returned for the unveiling of a plaque – organised by the Nottingham Railways Remembered group – commemorating the passage of fifty years since the station closed. The memorial is fixed to the side of the station clock tower which, itself, though dwarfed by the retail development, still looks magnificent. I wonder if that old hand-operated lift is inside it and if it still gives access to the subway which, I have heard, still runs beneath the site.

Nottingham Victoria with just a couple of years to go. B1 No. 61248 *Geoffrey Gibbs* waits in the gloom. (John Evans)

Summer Saturday

By John Cosford

I have very happy memories of the GCR, especially in Northamptonshire. I used to live in Northwood on the outer fringes of north-west London. Northwood was on the Metropolitan and GC line and so I can recall the 'Britannias', V2s, 'Royal Scots' and even BR Class 4 2-6-0s on the semi-fast trains to and from Marylebone. That all changed in mid-1962 with the closure of Neasden shed and the withdrawal of GC local stopping trains. One of the return semi-fast workings to Nottingham was replaced by a diesel multiple unit, which only left about three return steam workings and they were hauled by grubby LMS 'Black Five' 4-6-0s.

Luckily, I had some like-minded friends, one of whom had a car, and we started to explore the GC line north of Aylesbury. One summer Saturday in 1963 we found our way to Woodford Halse, about which we knew nothing, and were amazed by the activity there. We positioned ourselves on the road bridge south of the station and started photographing the many passing trains, which included lots of holiday extras as well as plenty of freights. The semaphore signals were flapping up and down at frequent intervals and sometimes it was hard to decide which way to point the camera! That was the first of a number of visits to Woodford and the surrounding area and I'm glad that we went there as the whole lot was gone within three years – very sad and a really stupid decision. Fortunately, there is still a lot of interest in the GCR, especially the London Extension.

Woodford Halse, Railway Town

The loss of a railway causes huge social and economic problems. Although the Great Central's London Extension existed for fewer than seventy years, it had a major impact on the towns and villages through which it passed. Nowhere was this more evident than at Woodford Halse, an isolated community in Northamptonshire that overnight became a sizeable railway community with engine sheds, freight yards, connecting services to two branch lines and prosperity that depended almost entirely on one industry.

As a journalist in the county, I wrote this article in 1973 – I am grateful to the *Northampton Chronicle and Echo* for permission to reprint it.

Facing the Facts in the Village that Lost its Railway

They say that Woodford Halse died when the railway closed.

Set in the heart of possibly the loveliest part of Northamptonshire, where the rolling uplands are punctuated by quiet, attractive villages, Woodford Halse was a railway community in just the same way as Crewe, Swindon or Derby, although on a smaller scale.

In the words of one retired railwayman, 'We had all our eggs in one basket. We never thought the line would close, and when it did there was nothing to replace it.'

Eight years have passed since the mammoth marshalling yards last echoed to the rattle of trucks being shunted. The mighty engine sheds, which sometimes housed up to fifty steam locomotives, have been pulled down and all the track has been removed.

So how has the village managed to reconcile itself to its new position?

The trouble that faced Woodford is that it owed its prosperity in too large a way to one industry. The village, which now has just under 2,000 inhabitants, has boasted in its time a cinema, four pubs, four churches and a very strong community spirit.

When the railway closed, all that survived was the British Railways Staff Association Club (converted from an old hunting hotel), which had been formed ten years earlier, four churches and one pub.

Typical of those who have witnessed the changes is Frank 'Sailor' Howes of 7A Pool Lane. He worked on the railways for thirty-four years and was lucky enough to retire on his sixty-fifth birthday; 12 June 1965 – the day the engine sheds closed.

The village seems more dead. The trouble started when the Great Central line through here changed from the Eastern Region to the London Midland Region. Our crack expresses were withdrawn from the Marylebone to Sheffield run and things just started to decline. I was a platelayer working on the tracks. The line was busy day and night because it was a junction for Banbury and Stratford-upon-Avon as well as having the main line. Now you can't get anywhere from here. We have lost our railways and we have lost our form of transport.

'You don't get the smoke, you don't hear the wagons clanking — but you don't meet people in the street...'

by John Evans

Facing the facts in a village that lost its railway

Mr Howes said Leicester was once one hour away by train.

> There was a lot of spirit among the railwaymen. I have railways in my blood and like many others, I thought it would never end. But it did, and there was no employment for the men when the worst happened.

Mr Reg Adams, who lives at 5 Castle Road, in the middle of the railway houses which border the high embankment, used to look after the carriage and wagon department.

He said that in his department alone there were eighty men. There were 700 there altogether when he retired in 1960. After that, he kept in close contact with everyone as president of the BR Staff Association Club, which thrived.

> What has changed? Well, you don't get smoke from the shed blowing up Castle Road and that can't be bad. And you don't hear the endless clanking of wagons in the yard. But you don't meet people in the street like you used to. At one time, with so many people coming off and going on shifts there was always someone in Woodford to talk to. Now you seldom meet people in the same way.

Mr Adams, a former parish councillor, said that the village was stunned by the closure of the railway, which happened in two months. But amazingly, Woodford picked itself up and made the best of the situation.

He recalled a parish meeting years ago when someone suggested the village should try to attract other industry. 'There wasn't even a seconder,' said Mr Adams.

The expected wholesale redundancies for the 450 men working on the railway at the time of closure never came. Many of the younger ones found new jobs before final closure. Others received a golden handshake, resulting in Woodford having a very high proportion of pensioners – nearly 1,000 of them in 1966.

The men who worked for the railways went many ways. Some headed to Banbury to continue working for the railways (and still do), but many found alternative employment. They went to Ford and British Timken at Daventry, Chrysler at Coventry, Export Packaging at Chipping Warden and Automotive Products at Leamington; few went to the Northampton side of Woodford to work.

Some men changed their jobs before finding one that suited them, but the only ones who had real trouble getting work were the senior drivers, who were among the higher wage earners at the depot. As they were around sixty years old, some of them had to take menial jobs such as sweeping up.

But Mr Adams thinks the village is more prosperous now than it was as a railway town. The line was once the main means of transport, but now many people have cars. The BR Club was taken over by the men who ran it in 1970 and is now a very successful social club open to all.

Mr T. Tudhope, of 19 Gorse Road, was a platelayer based at Woodford. He went to Banbury when the depot closed and although now retired, reiterated the general opinion that calls for new industry in Woodford. Although the railway has gone, it still has a physical presence. The overgrown track bed sweeps through platforms with no buildings. It heads over roads on bridges and on an embankment, past the site of the two huge marshalling yards and the now flattened engine sheds.

British Railways have not sold any of their land at Woodford. Mr Adams said that the derelict railway property, which goes right through the village, was an eyesore. There's nothing sentimental about the railways for most of those who used to work on the line.

British Rail and the Northamptonshire County Planning authority are at the moment co-operating to settle the future of the site. Among the questions still to be settled are how the embankments can be removed and the area landscaped. There seems little chance of the land quickly finding another use.

One point which seems to be restricting Woodford's ability to attract new industry is a lack of sewerage facilities. The parish council have protested to Daventry Rural Council about the sewage station, but so far nothing has been done.

There was an idea to build a large golf course on some of the land (well over 100 acres are lying abandoned) but at the time British Rail said they could not sell it. Recently there was a £100 million scheme for new housing, industry and open development, with some farming land and a country park.

Northamptonshire County Council think the railway has a moral responsibility to help to restore the land.

Others think British Rail were rash to tear down all the sheds in the first place. Landlord of the White Hart Mr Jim Vine thought the buildings could have been modified to serve some useful purpose.

Woodford used to depend on the railway for its livelihood; now it could depend on the railway land for its future.

(Reprinted from the *Northampton Chronicle and Echo*, 23 October 1973)

- The social club is still thriving in 2019 and has 700 members.
- A business park has now been created.
- The population in 2019 exceeds 3,500.
- There are currently two churches and one pub.
- A few bridges and other structures remain as a testament to Woodford's history.
- In 2034 the railway will have been closed for longer than it was open.

Every inch a railwayman: Mr Tudhope pictured in 1973. (*Northampton Chronicle and Echo*)

Keeping our Memories Alive

By Bryan Jeyes

It was never going to last. That last vestige of the London Extension – from Nottingham Arkwright Street to Rugby Central – was bound to close as soon as British Rail could get the necessary approvals in place. The forthcoming closure was announced by the late Richard Marsh – Minister of Transport – early in February 1969 and the final passenger trains ran on 3 May that year.

My college friend Adam Jones and I had regularly travelled over the line from Leicester to Nottingham, taking photographs in the process. In June of 1967 we had arranged a tour of Nottingham Victoria in order to photograph it before closure. It was therefore not surprising that the idea of making a record of the whole line to Rugby should start to germinate. Quite when the plan to make an audio recording as well appeared, I'm not sure, but I think it was crystallised by the visit of the, then, well-known broadcaster Charles Chilton to our college. He extolled the virtues of audio-visual presentations as a teaching aid, so off we went to make one with tape recordings and colour slides.

I had been given a Phillips portable cassette recorder for my twenty-first birthday a few months before. Not a professional bit of kit at all, but the results still sound surprisingly good. Adam, who was a drama student, consulted the relevant sections of George Dow's history of the line and prepared a commentary. He was careful not to make it intrusive as the purpose was to record the sound of the journey, but it highlighted points of interest and explained where we were.

On Saturday 8 February 1969, we stood in the street outside Arkwright Street station and started recording. Adam's introduction was followed by our ascending the staircase to the platform – with footfall rather heavier than necessary for dramatic effect – before emerging onto the platform with the familiar sound of the diesel multiple unit's engine ticking over. The front seats, behind the driver, were vacant and his compartment door was open. Amazingly the driver kept his door open throughout the journey, so we captured the cab sounds; the guard's buzzer, the horn and the brake applications.

There were few passengers and, in fact, at both East Leake and at Ashby Magna, Adam comments that nobody has left the train and no one has boarded it. Lutterworth was busier: three boys and a sledge! The sledge was explained by the fact that it had snowed overnight and this, together with the morning sunshine, made the gentle trundle through the countryside quite magical.

At Leicester Central the driver's curiosity got the better of him and he asked us what we were doing. There followed an impromptu recorded interview terminated only by the guard's repeated buzzing to indicate that we should be on our way!

At Rugby there were more heavy footsteps as we climbed to the booking hall on the Hillmorton Road. Adam delivered his closing words on the pavement, but he was drowned out by passing traffic, so we had to go back a week later and do a re-take. This time the echoing acoustics of the booking hall added to the occasion wonderfully.

Audio recording accomplished, our thoughts turned to the photographs. We had quite a few, but they mainly featured Leicester and Rugby Central stations and we wanted to illustrate the whole journey. So, when the line closed, I wrote to BR asking for permission to access the track. Amazingly they issued a walking permit for the length of the line. It restricted us to weekend activities but that didn't matter; so off in my faithful Austin A40 – which appears in some of the photos – we went.

Hindsight is, of course, wonderful and I simply don't know why some important features of the line are missing from our photographs; the crossing of the Midland line at Loughborough, for instance, and a track level view of the girder viaduct at Rugby where it crossed the LNWR line. Despite having a permit in my pocket, perhaps our nerve failed us!

In the end we selected about 140 photographs to accompany the audio recording, some of which appear in this book. There were two virtually identical sets to choose from because at most locations both Adam and I pressed the shutter. We were students and the equipment we used wasn't anything special, but it still yielded acceptable results. Adam's camera was a Kodak Retinette 1A, using mostly Kodachrome film, while I had an Ilford Sportsman loaded with Kodachrome or Ektachrome transparency film.

In the event, the AV presentation only had one public airing, to a ladies' group at Bishop Street Methodist Church in Leicester! It didn't get off to an auspicious start when the slide box was opened upside down, they all fell out and had to be hastily put back in something like the correct order before things could commence. In fact, it is only in the last few months that some sequencing errors stemming from that disaster have been corrected: I recently loaded the entire set on to a photo sharing site and people who know the line soon spotted the errors and assisted me in correcting them.

We made another full-length sound recording on the last train from Rugby Central to Arkwright Street, but it wasn't the same at all. The carriages were full of noisy chattering people; it was not the Great Central we had grown to love. That railway was much better summed up by the words Adam used to conclude the earlier recording in the echoing surroundings of Rugby Central's booking hall. They are from John Betjeman's poem 'Great Central Railway Sheffield Victoria to Banbury':

> And quite where Rugby Central is,
> Does only Rugby know,
> We watched the empty platform wait,
> And sadly saw it go.

Cutting the Wind –
The Standard 9Fs

Of the 251 Standard Class 9F 2-10-0s, no fewer than forty-one spent time allocated to Annesley shed for working freight on the Great Central. The first ones arrived in February 1957 when Nos 92067–92076 appeared, all having spent a short time at Doncaster. The fleet was disbanded in the summer of 1965, when the London Midland Region, having shifted Great Central freight services to other, less speedy lines, had to find homes for dozens of well run-in 9Fs. In the spring of 1965, Annesley still had twenty-three 9Fs on its books and it seems as though the very last to leave was No. 92043. Most disappeared during the summer of 1965, but No. 92043 was not moved to Burton until January 1966 according to official records.

Many of those that survived to the end had been delivered in 1957 and became very well known to linesiders.

The Eastern Region's fast freight service between Annesley and Woodford dates back to LNER days, initially as a slick and effective way of shifting coal from Nottinghamshire and South Yorkshire and steel from the Scunthorpe steel plant. With big freight yards at either end of the 70-mile section, the GC lent itself admirably to such an enterprise. It was a fast-flowing line, not too busy with passenger traffic and with few junctions to slow progress; it formed an excellent connection between the North East and the South West. Although it was a two-track line, lacking dedicated freight tracks, this worked to its advantage. It simply meant that the freights had to keep moving and the incentivised Great Central crews needed little encouragement to keep the speed up, despite many of the freights running without continuous braking. It was also a very effective use of manpower, as crews would be changed at Leicester to run out and home within their normal eight-hour working day.

Many of the freights went from Woodford to the SMJ line west to Stratford and Broom, or over the link to Banbury for forward progress.

The 9Fs revolutionised an already efficient service. With their propensity for free running, the 9Fs would haul sixty loaded wagons south and seventy empties north at speeds of up to 60 mph. Very little of the freight ended up on the GC itself, although some went to Ruddington, where there was a Ministry of Defence depot. There were also local freight trains serving stations on the route. But basically, it was coal, steel and mixed freight going one way, while the empties were worked just as fast in the return direction. Usually it was empties heading north, but some loaded freight also went in the Down direction. To someone used to seeing Midland line freights plodding their way between loops and complicated junctions (and using the same 9Fs), it was a revelation.

Apart from the unfitted 'windcutter' or 'runner' freights, the Great Central also carried a number of specialised or express freights, particularly the York–Bristol, which was always fully fitted. There were pick-up freights as well, serving local stations, and often hauled by an L1 tank or, later, a Stanier tank engine. Fish trains were also run over the Great Central, the Grimsby–Whitland (South Wales) train attracting special interest because it was usually hauled by a 'Britannia' from Immingham depot, which worked the train through to Banbury. As it left Grimsby in the late afternoon, we only saw this one in the summer months. Nos 70036–41 finally left Immingham in December 1963.

If you were really lucky you could catch a train with a pair of 9Fs up front. This was almost always a way of moving a 9F to where it was needed, rather than a train requiring exceptional power. Light engines were not that common, although photographer John Cosford caught one and it is reproduced here in this book. Author and photographer Colin Walker pointed out how the GC freights kept on moving, whatever the weather. I recall an example of this when arriving at Rugby Central one dismal morning, waiting for the four-car DMU to Nottingham. It was a freezing winter's day with the sort of fog that wraps itself around you, enveloping your senses. Just as our train was signalled, there was a roar from the station bridge and a 9F came speeding through the station, rods whirling and a hurricane draught scattering dust and leaves.

Most of the 9Fs at Annesley – and in early days, all of them – had the more capacious BR1F tender, one of which you can still see on the preserved No. 92212, but the Annesley engines never completely ruled the rails. It was not unusual to see a Western Region 9F at work and occasionally a Midland line 9F would be treated to a chance to show its speed capabilities by having a run on the Great Central. On a couple of occasions an ex-Crosti 9F appeared; John Cosford was also on hand to record this rare event.

The 9Fs were also used with success on passenger trains, although, as with the Western and Eastern Regions, the more ambitious drivers found such a free-running engine could be given its head and worked at speeds of 70 mph or more. Eventually there was a curb on speeds and the 9Fs were limited to 60 mph. Running them at high speeds meant excessive wear and reduced the time between workshop visits. Even so, right through to 1964 they could be found on excursions and even local passenger services. Compared with the 01 2-8-0s they replaced, themselves an expedient wartime rebuild of the old but very effective Great Central Railway 04 2-8-0, the 9Fs were faster, could haul heavier trains and required much less maintenance. Yet at one time Annesley had had fifty-one of these rebuilt 2-8-0s on its allocation.

The London Midland Region never tried to get the best out of the Great Central and while losing the express passenger trains in 1960 was a bitter

No. 92014 spent many years at Annesley. Now, in August 1965, its Great Central work is finished, and it is seen here at Canklow next to a Doncaster B1. (John Evans)

blow, the closure of the route to freight in 1965 signalled the end. By then, freight traffic was keeping the GC line alive and to visit Woodford with its vast yard empty and the engine shed bereft of locomotives was a very sad sight. Annesley kept its engine shed busy almost until the closure of the Great Central the following year, although Colwick took over for the final few months.

Today, as the rail routes to the north out of London get increasingly busy with passenger traffic – something we should all celebrate – it is getting very difficult to find paths for additional traffic. All of a sudden, a route that actually duplicates some of the busy current sections of line, such as from north London to Rugby, might have made sense if dedicated to freight use. Alas, it is too late. An unlikely plan to reopen a large section of the line for dedicated European freight in the early millennium years failed to get parliamentary support. Now the English Regional Transport Association has called for a section of the line to be reopened to provide a link from the Leicester–Nuneaton line to Calvert, for onward movement to north London, Oxford and Reading. This would be for freight and passenger traffic, to reduce pressure on the railways and the M1 and M40 motorways. Don't hold your breath.

The Lonely Signal

In the early 1970s I moved to live at Barby, on the Northamptonshire–Warwickshire border, a few miles south of Rugby. By then the Great Central was history, but I occasionally went for a walk along the track bed near Willoughby village. Here, the Great Central ran alongside the Grand Union canal and under the Willoughby to Barby road at a point near the old Navigation pub.

A few hundred yards on the way to Rugby, an old signal post, complete with signal arm, ladder and the access platform (with railings), still stood. Who knows why all the other signals and line side buildings had been removed, but this signal survived? As I had been attending an art class with a teacher who encouraged us to 'get outside and start drawing', I took my sketch pad along one day and made some careful pencil drawings of the old signal post and its surroundings.

Forty years later I found them in a box of watercolour paper and used them to create a picture, adding a northbound train. This signal was the Barby Up starter and about a mile farther south was Braunston and Willoughby station. Amazingly, when I passed over the old bridge a few years ago the signal was still there, now looking very dilapidated with the platform and railings hanging off precariously.

The 'Royal Scot' Saga

The real heroes of the 1948 locomotive exchanges, where the most significant types from pre-nationalisation days were tested against each other, were the LMS rebuilt 'Royal Scot' 4-6-0s. They performed outstandingly against their Class 8P competitors, such as the Great Western 'King', the LNER A4, the Southern 'Merchant Navy' Pacific and the LMS 'Coronation'. All these engines were significantly more powerful than the rebuilt 'Scot', but the LMS 4-6-0 really was the star of the show. If nationalisation had not happened, all the 'Patriots', 'Jubilees' and 'Royal Scots' would have been rebuilt. As it was, the final rebuild was No. 46137 in 1955. Only four years later, the advent of the first main line express diesels on the London Midland Region, the BR/Sulzer 'Peak' and the English Electric Type 4, played havoc with the lives of the rebuilt 'Scots', for they were in the same power class and set to work in large numbers. Displaced by English Electric Type 4s from West Coast route sheds like Willesden and Longsight, the 'Scots' offered a useful amount of extra power over the existing 'Jubilees' and a number of them found a new home on the Midland main line. This stay was not to be long, however. In 1962 the 'Peak' diesels took charge of most Midland line trains and once again there was a surplus of 'Royal Scots'. This time some were withdrawn, while others were again moved on. It was in that year that the rebuilt 'Scots' were allocated to the Great Central, the freight depot at Annesley eventually hosting seventeen Class 7P 4-6-0s.

This was not the first time 'Royal Scots' had run on the Great Central, as the 1961 FA Cup Final (Leicester lost 2-0 to a very strong Spurs team) saw the appearance of some of the class (and a rebuilt 'Patriot') temporarily based at Leicester Central shed, for working specials to Wembley. Polished up for these special workings, they gave no hint of what was to follow. Also, in 1962 No. 46128 *The Lovat Scouts* from Crewe North was an unusual visitor.

In May 1962, it was decided to allocate two 'Scots', Nos 46106 *Gordon Highlander* and 46118 *Royal Welch Fusilier*, to Leicester for working the Bournemouth–York through trains between Leicester Central and Banbury. These engines – especially No. 46118 – were in good condition but stayed only five weeks because the decision was made to run the train throughout with a Type 3 English Electric diesel.

Later that year the London Midland Region, needing power for the Manchester to Euston overnight sleeping car express and semi-fast services previously in the hands of Eastern V2 and B1 locomotives, started moving 'Royal Scots' to the Great Central. It is well documented that these were hardly the finest specimens of their type; the best examples were retained for the remaining work on the West Coast Main Line, with Annesley having to make do with those that were either requiring a major overhaul, something they would never get, or some kind of rectification. A classic example was No. 46143 *The South Staffordshire Regiment*. This weary engine had certainly put in the miles; by the time it arrived on the Great Central it had served no fewer than twenty-seven sheds in its illustrious career. By 1962 it had covered around 2 million miles and was two years out of a heavy overhaul; not in itself a problem, but like the others, it showed distinct signs of having fallen into disrepute. In the autumn of 1962, it was moved from Trafford Park at Manchester to Annesley, to become a particularly special thorn in the side of all who worked there. This locomotive was no longer the prized workhorse of various West Coast route sheds; she was unreliable, rough riding, often short of steam and clearly in need of major surgery. Yet, with her sisters, she worked the semi-fasts on the Great Central, plus the much heavier 11.15 Nottingham–London empty van train – a much more taxing assignment as it also conveyed empty newspaper vans, but hardly Shap with twelve on and no banker. The 'Scots' were also called upon to work freight. They even occasionally ended up double-heading with ex-Great Central o4 2-8-os on coal trains north of Nottingham. Using such a powerful locomotive with big driving wheels on lightweight trains or heavy freights was an uneconomic use of a dubious asset.

The servicing arrangements at the London end were also odd. The London Midland Region, in its wisdom, closed Neasden shed in June 1962. This meant that steam locomotives had to run to Cricklewood on the Midland main line for servicing. One or two ex-Midland line 'Royal Scots' found themselves back on familiar territory for a few hours while laying over in London.

It couldn't last. Maybe the LMR ran out of tired 7P 4-6-os with no work. Maybe Annesley said they would prefer the less complex and more suitable Black 5s. Gradually, the 'Royal Scots' were withdrawn and by late 1964 the saga was over. Incidentally, two other Class 7P engines also expanded the stud at Annesley. These were rebuilt 'Patriot' No. 45529 *Stephenson* and rebuilt 'Jubilee' No. 45535 *Comet*. Both joined the fun in October 1963 and the 'Jubilee' was among the last of the 7P 4-6-os to work on the Great Central as it was not retired until October 1964, by which time it was a rare survivor. It had been a fascinating time for Great Central enthusiasts; less so for those who had to work and maintain these once excellent, now unruly machines.

In June 1964 I arrived at Crewe station and watched the departure of an express for Glasgow. Expecting a diesel, I was delighted to find that the assigned locomotive was 'Royal Scot' No. 46155 *The Lancer* from Crewe North depot, with reasonably clean green livery and carrying polished nameplates. Despite the fact that she was seven years from a heavy general overhaul, she had been a regular visitor to Crewe Works for maintenance and the driver informed me she was a locomotive in 'good fettle'. *The Lancer* strode away confidently towards the northern hills with twelve coaches; the West Coast Main Line had saved the best for themselves.

It is hard to be exact about the details of when engines came and went. Engine record cards sometimes conflict with BR's published records and the observations of those who watched what was happening. My own research and memories suggest that claims by some people that Annesley improved the best examples, which were then promptly transferred to other depots, is almost certainly not the case. Nearly all the 'Royal Scots' which arrived at Annesley left for the scrapyard, sometimes via a 'paper' transfer to another depot. For example, No. 46165 *The Ranger (12th London Regt)* made the leap from Crewe North to Annesley appropriately on 29 February 1964. It was then moved back to Crewe North in November 1964 but was immediately withdrawn and sold to T. W. Ward of Beighton for scrap. Another interesting casualty was No. 46112 *Sherwood Forester,* one of the few British steam locomotives to be officially de-named, when Type 4 diesel No. D100 inherited her title. This engine was involved in a collision in March 1964 which severely damaged the front end. She lingered 'awaiting a decision on her future' which the humblest of trainspotters could have made. She was officially withdrawn at the end of April, having been a source of interest as she rested with a wrecked front end at Annesley, before being sold to Cashmore's at Great Bridge for scrap. By November 1964 the 'Royal Scot' saga was over.

Locomotive	Name	Arrived	Disposal	Notes
45529	*Stephenson*	October 1963	February 1964 – withdrawn	Withdrawn 22 February 1964. Scrapped at Crewe March 1964.
45735	*Comet*	12 October 1963	3 October 1964 – withdrawn	Withdrawn 3 October 1964 Scrapped at Cashmore's, Great Bridge.
46101	*Royal Scots Grey*	5 January 1963	31 August 1963 – withdrawn	Scrapped at Slag Reduction Co., Rotherham, April 1964.
46106	*Gordon Highlander*	12 May 1962 – Leicester Central	30 June 1962	Transferred to Saltley. Withdrawn from Carlisle Upperby 8 December 1962 but reinstated and worked on the Great Central in early 1963 before being withdrawn again. Scrapped at Crewe, April 1963.

Locomotive	Name	Arrived	Disposal	Notes
46111	*Royal Fusilier*	12 January 1963	28 September 1963 – withdrawn	Scrapped at Crewe, November 1963.
46112	*Sherwood Forester*	September 1962	9 May 1964 – withdrawn	Scrapped at Cashmore's Great Bridge, September 1964.
46114	*Coldstream Guardsman*	September 1963	28 September 1963 – withdrawn	Scrapped at Slag Reduction Co., Rotherham, April 1964.
46118	*Royal Welch Fusilier*	19 May 1962 – Leicester Central	30 June 1962	Transferred to Saltley.
46122	*Royal Ulster Rifleman*	December 1962	October 1964	Transferred to Carlisle, Upperby, but withdrawn when received on 17 October 1964. Scrapped at Draper's of Hull, February 1965.
46125	*3rd Carabinier*	October 1963	3 October 1964 – withdrawn	Scrapped at Cashmore's Great Bridge, January 1965
46126	*Royal Army Service Corps*	1 December 1962	5 October 1963 – withdrawn	Scrapped at Crewe, November 1963.
46143	*The South Staffordshire Regiment*	October 1962*	21 December 1963 – withdrawn	Scrapped at Crewe, January 1964.
46153	*The Royal Dragoon*	October 1962*	21 December 1962 – withdrawn	Scrapped at Crewe, May 1963.
46156	*The South Wales Borderer*	12 October 1963	10 October 1964 – withdrawn	Scrapped at Drapers of Hull, February 1965.
46158	*The Loyal Regiment*	September 1962*	19 October 1963 – withdrawn	Scrapped at Crewe, November 1963.
46163	*Civil Service Rifleman*	12 January 1963	29 August 1964 – withdrawn	Scrapped at Bird Group, Risca, February 1965

Locomotive	Name	Arrived	Disposal	Notes
46165	*The Ranger (12th London Regt.)*	29 February 1964	November 1964	Transferred to Crewe North but withdrawn when received on 21 November 1964. Scrapped at T. W. Ward of Beighton, March 1965.
46167	*The Hertfordshire Regiment*	21 September 1963	11 April 1964 – withdrawn	Scrapped at Crewe, May 1964.
46169	*The Boy Scout*	5 January 1963	25 May 1963 – withdrawn	Scrapped at Crewe, August 1963

Note: Scrapping dates are approximate.
*There is conflicting information among various official documents about this date.

Next stop Annesley. 'Royal Scot' *No. 46101 Royal Scots Grey* at Leighton Buzzard, reduced to working a down freight, prepares for a new life on the Great Central. (John Evans)

The Way Things Were

By Graham Onley

Most railway enthusiasts started their loco-spotting journey with no thought of where it might take them. We would have been too young to even contemplate such lofty thoughts! I was no exception, but I was lucky enough to be at the young end of our family line, three brothers and a sister having arrived before me. This luck led me, at a very early age, to become familiar with our Duston West, Northampton, patch and the railway surrounding the area, which was actually situated in the Far Cotton area of our very homely town.

I soon discovered that the all-consuming continuous aim was to get by any means possible to Blisworth or Roade, both nearby on the West Coast Main Line. Blisworth was not too difficult – there was a 4*d* (1.5p) train ride on the 'Blissy Flyer', but whenever we were lapping up the main line expresses, there was an uneasy feeling about what we might have missed on the freight lines at Roade, which went through Northampton to Rugby. Roade was further, but we occasionally reached Roade station by virtue of one of our number having a father who somehow never noticed our boarding his United Counties single-decker. We even had the luck to pick the right return trip.

Our main excitement was the number of Euston to Wolverhampton expresses designed to run via Northampton. In the early 1950s, 'Jubilees' from Bushbury shed monopolised these trains and it was not long before we wished for something more exotic. We came to sense that the British Railways Modernisation Plan of 1955 was likely to cut our steamy idyll short by some time in the 1970s. Events proved that we needed to widen our horizons rather earlier than that.

Our county was, we discovered, well blessed with a combination of both main lines and branch lines from north-east to south-west. One of the attractions was the 'old GC', as we called it, from Marylebone to Leicester, Nottingham, Sheffield and Manchester. This had been thrust into the arms of the London Midland Region with possibly unspoken instructions to close what had conveniently become a duplicate route. Like ripples in a pond, we spread out to discover more of what went on in distant parts of our county. By this time, cameras were the main part of our equipment.

I first visited the Great Central on Sunday 14 October 1962 to see B16 4-6-0 No. 61438 (from York) heading an enthusiasts' special from Marylebone to Derby Works as it passed Woodford Halse station. The day was wet and miserable with the Cuban Missile Crisis hanging in the wider world. More important to me at the time was the sight of Western Region 2-8-0 No. 2888 and Class 9F 2-10-0 No. 92003 from Cardiff East Dock. One of our number had arranged for his father to drive us to Woodford and the driver was more interested in the midday Sunday pub opening than the special. Later that day we saw another special, headed by Patriot No. 45543 *Home Guard* at Northampton.

On 30 November 1963 I was again by the Great Central lineside, this time further north to obtain a colour shot of a fast goods that we discovered too late was part of the fare on offer by the GC. No. 92116 headed Down empties on a day when black and white would have been preferable to the *2s 6d* (12.5p) cost of a colour slide. I managed to obtain an afternoon's leave on 25 February 1964 to again be at Woodford station when No. 4468 *Mallard* in almost LNER condition was due to be towed south for incarceration in Clapham Transport Museum. I was actually hoping to have sight of a 'Royal Scot', some of which clung to life working from Annesley shed on Nottingham–Marylebone semi-fast workings. Photographs were also obtained of Nos 5992 *Horton Hall*, 92005 (50A), 42250 (1G) – Woodford's final shed code – and 73000 (1G), all on shed.

Mallard eventually turned up later than expected and towed by Class 5 No. 73045 in pitch black conditions, which wasted some Kodachrome 2 transparencies. The highlight of the afternoon was the sight of one of our beloved 'Royal Scots', No. 46156 *The South Wales Borderer*, on a Down Nottingham train.

Our last visit to the GC was on the final day of normal operations. We took an electric multiple unit from Northampton to Rugby Midland and walked to Rugby Central station, taking advantage of the open house atmosphere. I sadly photographed a Class 5 followed by what is today an admittedly nostalgic diesel multiple unit running to Nottingham. I then photographed No. 45267 (2D) as it arrived light engine from Banbury and stabled its semi-fast to Nottingham Victoria. No. 45292 then appeared on a southbound parcels train – a welcome visitor as it had been a resident at Northampton from 1954 to 1960. By the time we had to hurry away to play in a Northampton Town League soccer match, the last visitor had passed through – No. 35030 *Elder Dempster Lines* on another enthusiasts' special.

I now know much more of the history of the old GC than I did then. I am acutely aware what the year of my birth cost me in terms of appreciating what could have been a far more valuable line than time allowed. Imagine if it had clung on a couple of decades longer ...

'The greatest coup in history!'

'Earth was not created in a day, nor will it ever be recorded that officials of the Main Line Preservation Group pulled off the greatest coup in history.' So wrote Richard Willis in the autumn 1969 issue of *Main Line*, the second to be published. He was chairman of the MLPG and its mission was undoubtedly the most ambitious in the preservation world at the time – to preserve a generous section of main line in the East Midlands. 'Within a few months we shall all know the outcome of our endeavours,' he predicted.

In January 1970 the nascent group took possession of Loughborough Central station. Richard Willis wrote in issue 4, published in autumn 1970:

> In early spring, our proposition was put to the Railways Board for the purchase of the track and land between Leicester (Abbey Lane sidings) and Loughborough Central station, inclusive of all structures and accessories. No track lifting has taken place between these two points nor, indeed, north to Ruddington, which is still our ultimate aim.

As a journalist on a local evening newspaper, I was invited to see the Great Central Railway preservation scheme in its early days, meeting with Richard and Graham Oliver on 18 March 1973. With an industrial tank engine shuttling about, it seemed a far cry from the Great Central we knew in the 1960s. But never underestimate a group of enthusiasts on a mission. With locomotives and rolling stock arriving regularly, there was a fascinating build-up to the running of the first trains on 30 September 1973, with a few ups and downs on the way. There was no doubting the determination of the early pioneers as they launched services between Loughborough and Quorn and Woodhouse over some rather weedy double track. That wasn't the only problem those pioneers faced. A printed slip in issue No. 12 of *Main Line* magazine apologised for the delay in publication due to 'the government's emergency regulations'. It was a time of strikes, oil embargoes and general instability, but Willis and his team pushed through it all. The trust members never forgot the Great Central's earnest motto, 'Forward.' They would be impressed to know that the Leicester–Ruddington dream is alive and well and within touching distance.

The End of the Line

A large congregation of railway enthusiasts, townsfolk and other interested persons witnessed the last rites of the Great Central Railway between Aylesbury and Rugby on Saturday.

The mourners were at Brackley station. The last train to use the station was due at midnight, but a railway enthusiasts' excursion from Waterloo to Sheffield and Marylebone was passing through the station earlier in the evening and it was this express which the enthusiasts had turned up to see.

As the crowd patiently waited, some of the flowers which adorned the station were clipped, while others were dug up from the roots. It was a very sad occasion.

The station staff then joined the crowd, and at last a shrieking whistle was heard out of the dusk. There was a clatter of whirling side rods as a Southern Region express locomotive named *Elder Dempster Lines* roared through the station with its trail of green and one red coaches.

The mourners stood in silence as the train hurried away into the darkness over Brackley viaduct, whistling again.

Slowly the crowd dispersed and those who had come from some distance away (one person had driven from Salisbury for the occasion) drove off.

For west Northamptonshire residents, this was the end of the line. Farewell Great Central – we shall miss you. (Reprinted from the *Northampton Chronicle and Echo*, 5 September 1966 with thanks. The author wrote this when he worked there as a junior reporter).

Last Word

By Rob Govier

What on earth was this? There was an occasional advertisement in *Railway Magazine* showing an A3 at full power, and some intriguing words about preserving a line from Leicester to Nottingham. Dreams or a potential reality? I was sceptical.

The Great Central dipped gracefully down on a grand embankment from the south Nottinghamshire uplands into Loughborough, visible from the more mundane Midland Main Line. It seemed aloof and mysterious. Was this the line intended to be a preserved railway like no other?

Finally, the optimistic adverts were replaced by news items in the railway press about open days at Loughborough Central, maybe even live steam. The name 'Main Line Steam Trust' seemed grandiose. Clearly something was happening, and it was time to investigate.

In February 1973 I scrambled up the trackless embankment just south of Loughborough Midland, and kept walking towards London. There must be a station somewhere. First came twin buffer stops, a bracket signal shorn of its arms, and eventually, the unmistakable shape of a Bulleid Pacific sheltering under a bridge. The track was in an elegant, lazy-radiused curve heading towards the platforms at Loughborough Central, where an industrial loco simmered and a Black Five sulked lifeless. Clearly the early stages of new life.

This railway needed volunteers and after a few regular visits in March 1973, aged twelve, I obtained an ex-BR station foreman's cap, dark jacket, and dispensed 2p tickets for footplate rides. Easter 1973 saw the platforms full of visitors and a brake van offered the very first passenger transport on the line since closure. Something beyond dreams and rusted track had begun.

More stock arrived, including the splendid, pampered *King Haakon 7*, jealously protected by its wealthy owner from Saffron Walden, often wearing a genuine NSB uniform. Various industrials with strange names: *Lamport No. 3*, *Hilda*, *Barrington Marston*, *Thompson* and *Evershed*. Odd machines such as a weary looking Sentinel, incongruously named after a pretty harbour town, St Monans, in Fife.

Throughout summer 1973 there was an optimism that matched the season, an enjoyment of achievement, hope for a bright future, fulfilment of the dreams of the pioneers, trains escaping the yard onto the long stretches of high-speed railway south towards Leicester. Indeed, things would get much better later in autumn. On the other hand, unforeseen at the time, disappointment awaited at the end of the year.

Unbeknown to us pioneer volunteers, the all-important numbers simply didn't add up. Revenue from open days fed precious little into the trust's coffers. Furthermore, there was a significant recurring cost which added no immediate value to the railway. 'Track Interest' was a euphemism for what seemed to be mafia-style protection money. The Great Central had been re-laid at the end of the 1950s, and the barely worn flat-bottomed rail was a significant asset to the British Railways Board, immediately reusable elsewhere on the network. The proposition from BRB was stark – unless you pay £1,100 per month (£13,100 today!), we will lift the track.

The original vision of running into Leicester Central had been scaled back to Abbey Lane sidings, 2 miles north, then further back to just south of Belgrave and Birstall. North of Loughborough, Nottingham became unreachable. BR were going to use the line for the foreseeable future to serve a strategic MoD depot at Ruddington, accessing it through a new chord at Loughborough. A door firmly shut. Therefore, the financially crippling track interest did not even cover the originally envisioned line. Sales of 2p footplate ride tickets weren't going to offset this. What next?

A lobster-bake. This was an event involving lobsters flown in from the USA, and invitations went to potential wealthy donors and backers, plus key officials from the local BR division. It was bizarre, creative, but sadly not effective. The concept was a journey from Loughborough to Quorn on the immaculate NSB coach hauled by *King Haakon*, a posh seafood barbecue, wining and dining with a view to soliciting funds. An enjoyable day out, but ultimately fruitless, except in one key aspect.

As a result of this junket, local BRB officials were so impressed by the levels of professionalism that they gave permission for passenger services to operate to Quorn. The dormant 'Black Five' was finally steamed, two ex-BR coaches arrived, and on 30 September services commenced. Thus, we went from shuffling tank locos to a passable main line service within nine months. We were duly proud. Sadly, it wasn't to last.

It had been overlooked that MLST were actually operating trains on the BR network with unsupervised amateurs. However, liability for any incident still lay with BR. The Department for the Environment, successor to the Department of Transport, acted swiftly. One Saturday morning, station staff arrived to find that there were no trains to dispatch.

It was a game of snakes and ladders. We had achieved so much in a single year. Now we seemed to have gone down a very large snake. Coincidentally, several locos failed boiler tests, including the flagship Black Five. Hence the only motive power serviceable was a small diesel shunter which gave brake van rides along the Loughborough site. Not main line, nor steam. Even this loco was to fail. The mood on the railway matched the national mood of gloom. Power cuts and a three-day week loomed. Things could only get better, but it would take a long time, and further setbacks awaited.

Had we recreated 'Watkin's Folly' as the GCR's detractors had often called the line – ambitious aims with no commercial foundation? We had to wait and see; and it was a long wait.

An unidentified BR Standard Class 5 4-6-0 passing under the SMJ line on the approach to Woodford Halse with a through train from the Southern Region on 10 August 1963. (John Cosford)

BR Class 9F 2-10-0 No. 92021 from Kettering crossing the viaduct over Swithland Reservoir with an Up freight train. This locomotive was one of ten that started life with Crosti boilers, and they were a rare sight on the Great Central. (John Cosford)

LMS Fairburn 2-6-4T No. 42250 leaving Woodford Halse with a local train to Banbury on 22 October 1963. It is passing the spur to the Stratford-upon-Avon line. (John Cosford)

Woodford Halse during the calm before the storm. A WD 2-8-0 is taking the main line rather than branching off to the Stratford route. (British Railways London Midland Region).

WD 2-8-0 No. 90103 at Nottingham Victoria, on 18 April 1964, with a Down train of iron ore halted at signals. It was allocated to Colwick shed. (John Cosford)

1964 – The 'Royal Scot' saga. LMS 'Royal Scot' 4-6-0 No. 46163 *Civil Service Rifleman* enters the north end of Nottingham Victoria station with empty stock for the 17:15 semi-fast passenger train to Marylebone. (John Cosford)

Class O4/8 2-8-0 No. 63675 with a Down freight train halted at signals at Nottingham Victoria station on 18 April 1964. Having served in France in the 1914–18 war, it was eventually rebuilt twice and gave forty-eight years' service before withdrawal in January 1966. (John Cosford)

Gresley V2 2-6-2 No. 60932 crossing the viaduct over Swithland Reservoir with an Up parcels train on 18 April 1964. No-one was bothered about the photographer being here – happy days! (John Cosford)

A rear three-quarter view of BR 9F 2-10-0 No. 92031 with an Up freight, passing through Nottingham Victoria station on 18 April 1964. This engine was allocated to Annesley shed from 1957 to the end of freight working in 1965. (John Cosford)

Ivatt Class 4 2-6-0 No. 43064 from Colwick arriving at Nottingham Victoria's platform 7 with a local train from Derby Friargate on 18 April 1964. (John Cosford)

The sad sight of LMS 'Royal Scot' 4-6-0 No. 46112 *Sherwood Forester* dumped at Annesley shed with a damaged front end in April 1964. This resulted from a collision the previous month at Woodhouse Mill, near Sheffield. Notice the ominous gallows-like structure in the background. (John Cosford)

Class 9F 2-10-0 No. 92006 at the southern end of Charwelton water troughs with a Down mixed freight on 25 July 1964. This engine was allocated to York shed. (John Cosford)

'Royal Scot' 4-6-0 No. 46156 *The South Wales Borderer*, with the 17:15 Nottingham to Marylebone passenger train, takes water at Charwelton water troughs on 25 July 1964, three months before withdrawal. (John Cosford)

English Electric Type 3 diesel No. D6798 passes the closed Charwelton station with the Down Bournemouth–York passenger train on 8 August 1964. Notice the long row of stored mineral wagons and the exchange sidings on the right for the nearby ironstone quarry. (John Cosford)

BR 9F 2-10-0 No. 92030 running light engine on the Up line near Wolfhampcote, south of Rugby, on 8 August 1964. It was probably running light engine to Woodford Halse to pick up an unbalanced Down freight working. (John Cosford)

A3 No. 4472 *Flying Scotsman* races through Culworth with a southbound rail tour on 18 April 1964, the photographer having endured a long cycle ride to obtain this picture. (Graham Onley)

Restored to LNER condition, No. 4468 *Mallard* is towed south through Woodford on what was expected to be its last journey on 25 February 1964. It was bound for Clapham Transport Museum. The non-corridor tender is correct for the engine when it was new. (Graham Onley)

The very first Standard Class 5, No. 73000, spent more than two years allocated to Woodford in the 1960s and is seen here at its home shed in 1964. (Graham Onley)

Stand clear! 'Royal Scot' No. 46156 *The South Wales Borderer* heads towards Woodford on a southbound semi-fast on 25 February 1964. (Graham Onley)

A charming portrait on 18 April 1964 of Culworth station, already closed, but showing the typical GC layout and elegant over bridge. (Graham Onley)

A Colwick-based B1 4-6-0, No. 61188, stands at Nottingham Victoria station on 2 August 1965 as station pilot with a rake of parcels vans. On the right is a DMU that has arrived from Marylebone on the 08:38, which we had caught at Rugby Central. Victoria is starting to look a bit shabby as the unwanted stepchild of the disinterested London Midland Region. (John Evans).

LMS Stanier 'Black Five' 4-6-0 No. 45406 seen south of Lutterworth with the 08:15 semi-fast from Nottingham Victoria to Marylebone, 24 April 1965. (John Cosford)

Stanier 'Black Five' 4-6-0 No. 45406 crossing the River Soar north of Loughborough with the 14:38 semi-fast passenger train from Marylebone to Nottingham Victoria on 24 April 1965. (John Cosford)

Mansfield Central station on the former Mansfield Railway between Kirkby South Junction and Clipstone Junction, a line that was worked from the start in 1917 by the Great Central. Scheduled passengers' services were withdrawn in 1956 but the station remained open for excursion traffic until closure in 1962. Despite the impressive size of the buildings, it had wooden platforms. It was finally demolished in 1972. (John Cosford)

With a good head of steam and safety valves lifting, Stanier 'Black Five' 4-6-0 No. 44765 heads south out of Aylesbury with the 08:15 semi-fast train from Nottingham to Marylebone on 3 July 1965. On the right are the stabling sidings for the Aylesbury–Marylebone commuter DMUs. (John Cosford)

Class EM2 Co-Co No. 27006 *Pandora* and EM1 No. 26034 on a freight at Sheffield Victoria on 5 August 1965. Notice the bulky pantographs. No. 27006 is painted blue but has no yellow warning panel. (John Evans)

Woodford Halse motive power depot from the north on 27 August 1966 after closure. The nearest building on the right is the machine shop and the gabled building behind is the carriage and wagon repair shop. On the left is the running shed. (John Cosford)

Power for the journey to Rugby Central on the 16:38 to Nottingham is this grubby Colwick Class 5, No. 44825, seen here at Woodford. Although it kept time, the driver was out at every station inspecting the motion. The GC was in its dying days. This was 7 April 1966. (John Evans)

On 26 March 1966, B1 No. 61302, very nicely turned out, has just coupled up and gets ready to leave Colwick with the RCTS Eight Counties Railtour. This train started at Northampton and ran to Leicester, Nottingham, Sheffield, Woodhead, Crewe and back to Northampton using a Class 24, an 8F, a B1, electric No. 26000 *Tommy*, 'Jubilee' No. 45596 *Bahamas* and an AC electric. No. 61302 was withdrawn the next day. (John Evans)

On 12 November 1966, Leicester Central (a spacious, main line station) had been reduced to an unstaffed halt for local trains between Rugby Central and Nottingham following closure of the Great Central as a through route. This sad view shows signal arms missing and no-one in sight. It's hard to imagine an A3 halting here with the Up 'Master Cutler' for Marylebone. (John Evans)

On 4 April 1966 a Class 5 4-6-0 heads south on the Great Central. The train is the 11:15 Nottingham–Marylebone parcels and it has just passed under the bridge carrying the Blisworth–Stratford line over the GCR. The Class 5 has a heaped tender but was making a dreadful clanking noise from its motion. (John Evans)

Helmdon Viaduct, with the Northampton & Banbury Junction Railway from Towcester to Banbury passing beneath on 19 March 1966. This is one of many handsome viaducts built by the GC. Some have been demolished, but this one survives. (John Evans)

A DMU for Aylesbury Town leaving South Aylesbury Halt on 31 May 1966, part of the old Great Western & Great Central Joint Railway created in 1906. The halt was closed in June 1967. (Bryan Jeyes)

A white MGB heads a line of interesting cars seen at Aylesbury Town station car park on 31 May 1966. In those days most larger stations had a red telephone box. (Bryan Jeyes)

The simple yet elegant buildings at Aylesbury Town station on 31 May 1966. (Bryan Jeyes)

Aylesbury South on 11 November 1967. This signal box is now at Swithland Sidings on the revived GCR. (Bryan Jeyes)

The very end of steam as 2-8-0 No. 48170 is at Nottingham Victoria on 8 October 1966, heading towards Ruddington. (Bryan Jeyes)

This is the point where the Great Central crosses the Banbury–Bletchley line at Brackley. It wouldn't be long before both lines disappeared on 9 April 1966. (John Evans)

Black 5 No. 45190 waits at the buffer stops at Marylebone, after arriving from Nottingham. (Bryan Jeyes)

Carrington was the first station north of Nottingham Victoria and one of the few without an island platform on the London Extension of the Great Central. (Bryan Jeyes)

A diesel multiple unit leaves Rugby Central on the last day of through working, 3 September 1966. (Graham Onley)

Black 5 No. 45267 stands at Rugby Central on the last day of the full London Extension, 3 September 1966. When Annesley shed closed, the locomotive moved to Wigan for another year's service. (Graham Onley)

Nottingham London Road High Level, with Brush Type 4 No. D1820 passing through heading mineral wagons in June 1967. (Bryan Jeyes)

The last day special near Rugby Central behind 'Merchant Navy' Class 4-6-2 No. 35030 *Elder Dempster Lines*, the final express to run on the Great Central. (Graham Onley)

Nottingham Victoria with a Sulzer Type 2 in attendance on 8 October 1966. Only local trains to Grantham and Rugby used Victoria at this date. (Bryan Jeyes)

New Basford station, Nottingham, on the Great Central line between Carrington and Bagthorpe Junction, photographed on 8 October 1966. The station closed to passengers in September 1964 but remained open for goods until October 1967. (Bryan Jeyes)

A snowy day at Woodford Halse in January 1967, four months after closure. Demolition awaits. (Bryan Jeyes)

Brackley Central station looking north on 16 July 1967 and still pretty much intact ten months after closure. The grassy level section to the left of the track was the site of a platform for a proposed branch line from Brackley to Northampton, which was never built. (John Cosford)

Leicester Central is now a huge unstaffed halt. A diesel multiple is at the platform, but business looks scarce. Taken in April 1967. (Bryan Jeyes)

Nottingham Victoria's elegant booking hall on 3 December 1966. The British Railways Board notice undoubtedly spells more bad news. (Bryan Jeyes)

Nottingham Victoria in 1967 – empty platforms, the clock still runs and signals optimistically suggest trains will be coming. (Bryan Jeyes)

A ticket window, one of seven. In his quest to record some of the more intriguing details of the old station, Bryan Jeyes captured the words 'Great Central' over the ticket window, no doubt a survivor from when the station was opened nearly seventy years earlier. (Bryan Jeyes)

A smart Cravens diesel multiple unit seen at Rugby Central on 22 April 1967 with a Nottingham local. From this angle not much has changed since the end of through services. (Bryan Jeyes)

Culworth Junction signal box after the scrap merchants had burned it down in order to access the metal lever frame inside on 16 July 1967. (John Cosford)

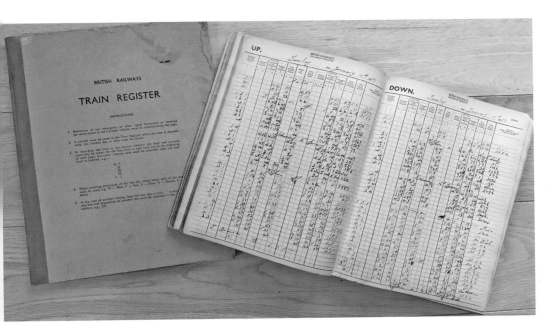

When the line was abandoned in 1966, I visited Eydon Road signal box on the Woodford–Banbury line; this closed along with the GC main line. Knowing the demolition men would destroy everything, I grabbed the Train Registers for the 1950s, which I still have today. They make fascinating reading, with a number of Western Region RODs making the trip towards their spiritual home, the GC. (John Evans)

Nottingham Victoria in June 1967, shortly before the end of services. This view shows its elegant, lofty interior, actually a huge 'double island' station with twelve platforms. A diesel unit can be seen on the left. (Bryan Jeyes).

Nottingham Victoria's platform 6 clings to life with staircase and adverts in June 1967. Three months to go until complete closure. (Bryan Jeyes)

Another delightful cameo. This beautiful clock over a doorway shows the exquisite detail rendered by Victorian craftsmen at Victoria station. (Bryan Jeyes)

Cornice mouldings inside the station –
what a sad thought that all this would be
rubble in a few weeks. (Bryan Jeyes)

Nottingham London Road High Level with a diesel unit for Grantham in the platform.
(Bryan Jeyes)

Nottingham Victoria. A signal, turntable and weeds in June 1967. (Bryan Jeyes)

Weekday Cross Junction. The line from Victoria station comes out of a tunnel to the left. The Grantham line curves off to the left of the signal box while the ex-Great Central main line to London goes straight ahead. By the time of this photograph in June 1967 only a truncated service to Rugby Central used the old main line. (Bryan Jeyes)

Nottingham Victoria south end with demolition in progress on 27 September 1967. (Bryan Jeyes)

Demolition starting at Nottingham Victoria immediately after closure in September 1967. (Bryan Jeyes)

Nottingham Victoria with a lonely chimney and roof structure exposed by the demolition gang. (Bryan Jeyes)

The splendid clock tower with surrounding buildings already being taken down on 27 September 1967. (Bryan Jeyes)

Two weeks later and now the clock tower stands alone, with the clock still working. (Bryan Jeyes)

Workmen attacking the old station – soon there will be little left to reflect upon. (Bryan Jeyes)

A general view on a sunny autumn day shows that half the station has been dismantled and the rest will not last long in the quest for more shopping space. (Bryan Jeyes)

The first tracks are lifted, and wagons are present to haul away the rubble. A last view of the station more or less intact in September 1967. (Bryan Jeyes)

By February 1968 demolition of the remaining structure is proceeding apace. Those newly laid rails won't be needed for very long. (Bryan Jeyes)

On the Down platform at Rugby Central, business looks brisk, with a train arriving to form a service for Nottingham and another in the sidings. Taken on 22 April 1967. (Bryan Jeyes)

Sheffield Victoria station and the Royal Victoria Hotel on 18 November 1967. (Bryan Jeyes)

Leicester Central station in 1967 looking deserted. (Bryan Jeyes)

In June 1967, a Brush Type 4 heads a freight through Nottingham London Road High Level, which is beyond Weekday Cross Junction on the Grantham line. (Bryan Jeyes)

Class EM2 No. 27006 *Pandora* at Sheffield Victoria station on 18 November 1967. (Bryan Jeyes)

The end of the line. Class EM1 No. 26049 at Manchester Piccadilly in July 1968. In Great Central days the station was known as London Road. Even the electrified section of the Great Central main line came under threat and was closed in 1981 after a life of less than thirty years. (Bob Mullins)

We are now on a journey with Bryan Jeyes and Adam Jones over the line as it existed in 1969 and 1970 (see text). This is Nottingham Arkwright Street station with its unprepossessing entrance by the man behind the cyclist. (Adam Jones)

The platforms at Arkwright Street – a pretty dowdy station. It closed in 1963, was reopened in 1967 when Victoria closed and finally shut its doors in 1969. (Bryan Jeyes)

The Great Central main line heading through Nottingham towards Victoria from Arkwright Street. (Bryan Jeyes)

Goods no more. The GC specialised in impressive viaducts as, coming late to the party, it had to pass over all the existing cityscapes. This one takes the main line over the River Trent. (Bryan Jeyes)

The Great Central near Wilford, with Roland Green school on the right. (Bryan Jeyes)

Wilford brick works and signal box viewed from Ruddington Lane. (Bryan Jeyes)

Ruddington station platforms and signal box looking south in 1970. The station was closed to passengers in 1963 and subsequently demolished. (Adam Jones)

Shallow cuttings and elegant bridges defined the GC's London Extension, pictured perfectly here between Ruddington and Gotham in August 1969. (Bryan Jeyes)

The old signal at Gotham sidings.
(Adam Jones)

Rushcliffe Halt and gypsum works looking north in March 1970. This section of line remained open at the time to serve the MoD depot. (Adam Jones)

East Leake station with its tired-looking buildings in March 1970, a few months after closure. (Adam Jones)

The GC viaduct over the River Soar. The viaduct was built and then the river diverted to pass beneath it. (Adam Jones)

Loughborough Central station in late 1969 before the preservationists moved in. (Bryan Jeyes)

A view looking north at Loughborough Central in October 1969. (Bryan Jeyes)

A desolate-looking Quorn and Woodhouse station in September 1969. (Adam Jones)

A diesel multiple unit on the Great Central at Kinchley Lane, near Swithland, in April 1969. (Adam Jones)

Immaculate permanent way at Swithland Reservoir in late 1969. (Adam Jones)

A diesel unit crosses Swithland Reservoir in April 1969, on the most scenic part of the current GC route, but this was in the last days of BR. (Bryan Jeyes)

Rothley station on a wintry-looking day in April 1969. (Adam Jones)

The one that got away. Belgrave and Birstall station in June 1969 looking towards the site of what is now Leicester North. (Adam Jones)

Rusty rails and classic Great Central buildings. Belgrave and Birstall station in June 1969. (Adam Jones)

Abbey Lane sidings in March 1969, viewed from Parker Lane, Leicester. (Bryan Jeyes)

The main line north of Leicester Central. (Bryan Jeyes)

Leicester Passenger North box in June 1969. (Bryan Jeyes)

The 11:02 to Nottingham departs from a deserted Leicester Central station. (Adam Jones)

Leicester Central, but everything is closed as it is now unstaffed. (Bryan Jeyes)

A multiple unit arrives from Rugby under the well-known linked water columns at Leicester Central on 29 April 1967. (Bryan Jeyes)

A familiar view at the south end of Leicester Central, but by June 1969 only one signal remains. (Bryan Jeyes)

Leicester engine shed (38C), still standing five years after closure. Once the home of A3s and V2s, it became 15E when transferred to the London Midland Region in February 1958 and then closed in 1964. A historic picture. (Bryan Jeyes)

Leicester South Goods in June 1969, a location regularly featured by Colin Walker in his definitive books on the Great Central. (Bryan Jeyes)

The Great Central crossing over the Leicester to Nuneaton line north of Whetstone. (Adam Jones)

Whetstone station, overgrown but still basically complete six years after trains last called there. (Adam Jones)

Ashby Magna station, its tall lattice signal gaunt and redundant. (Bryan Jeyes)

Ashby Magna station, which survived to the very end of passenger services between Rugby and Nottingham. (Bryan Jeyes)

The fledgling M1 motorway, bereft of traffic, alongside the rusty Great Central north of Lutterworth in June 1969. (Bryan Jeyes)

This is Lutterworth, which I can recall as a busy station in its day. A train for Nottingham has unloaded a few passengers in April 1969. Time is running out fast for these trains. (Bryan Jeyes)

The subway at Lutterworth in its last days, with broken windows over the stairway and an extraordinary lamp. (Bryan Jeyes)

We have now reached Rugby, and this is the big girder bridge over the West Coast Main Line, which V2s and 9Fs crossed at indecent speeds. (Adam Jones)

The northern approach to Rugby Central with more rusty rails. (Adam Jones)

The ticket office at Rugby Central station after closure. Just another old station awaiting the demolition men. But how many wonderful journeys started here? (Adam Jones)

Rugby Central station was positioned on an over bridge about fifteen minutes' walk from Rugby Midland. Notice the gables, the phone box and the BR Board's withdrawal of services sign. By this time, despite the welcoming open door, it was closed for business. (Bryan Jeyes)

On 1 March 1973 No. 6024 *King George I* left Barry scrapyard for Quainton Road station, Buckinghamshire, where a nascent preservation centre was being set up. Here she is the following month, on 27 April 1973. She looks in good order, but it was to be 1990 before this engine ran again. (John Evans)

Nottingham Midland beneath the huge Great Central overbridge, which dominated the station in those days. 'Peak' No. D87 prepares to move off with the Down 'Thames Clyde Express' on 19 May 1973. The Midland Railway must have loved having that bridge built over their station, but they had the last laugh. (John Evans)

A nice bright November day in 1973 at the Great Central Railway's Loughborough headquarters. Here we have 0-6-0T No. 39 taking water. (John Evans)

In the 1970s, freight trains were still using the remaining single track of the Great Central north of Loughborough from time to time. On this occasion I got lucky with my camera. I was near the closed East Leake station and this train came past with a very unusual load, including trucks, old Land Rovers and well-used cars. I assume the service was for the MoD at Ruddington. (John Evans)

At Helmdon, there is a haunting – almost mystical – feeling while viewing the empty wide cuttings of the GCR, something not always felt about other lines that have long been closed. (Bob Mullins)

Bibliography

Betjeman, J., *Collected Poems* (London, John Murray, 1988)

Longworth, H., *BR Steam Locomotives 1948–1968* (Hersham, Ian Allan, 2014)

Madox Ford, F., *The Good Soldier* (Ware, Wordsworth Classics, 2010)

Pearce, D., *Rugby to Loughborough* (Midhurst, Middleton Press, 2012)

Sixsmith, I., *The Book of the Patriots* (Clophill, Irwell Press Ltd, 2003)

Sixsmith, I., *The Book of the Royal Scots* (Clophill, Irwell Press Ltd, 2008)

Walker, C., *Main Line Lament* (Oxford, Oxford Publishing Co., 1973)

Walker, C., *Great Central Twilight* (Llangollen, Pendyke Publications,1986)

Walker, C., *Great Central Twilight Finale* (Llangollen, Pendyke Publications, 1993)

Magazines (various issues)

Modern Railways

Trains Illustrated

Railway Magazine

Steam Days (September 2019)

Main Line (issues 3–12)

Chris Ward's Annesley Website: http://www.annesleyfireman.com (2019) [Accessed 25 October 2019]